LET YOUR
PAST
BE YOUR PLATFORM

LET YOUR PAST BE YOUR PLATFORM

Jarrod Dunn

Let Your Past Be Your Platform Copyright © 2016 by Jarrod Dunn. All rights reserved. This book or any portion thereof may not be reproduced or used in any manner whatsoever without the express written permission of the publisher except for the use of brief quotations in a book review.

Although the author and publisher have made every effort to ensure the information in this book was correct at press time, the author and publisher do not assume and hereby disclaim any liability to any party for any loss, damage, or disruption caused by errors or omissions, whether such errors or omissions result from negligence, accident, or any other cause. Views expressed in this publication do not necessarily reflect the views of the publisher.

www.jarroddunn.comwww.jarroddunn.com

jarroddunn@yahoo.com
Printed in the United States of America
First Printing, 2016
ISBN 978-1-941749-63-0

4-P Publishing
Chattanooga, TN 37411

CONTENTS

Introduction 7
Forgiveness 11
   Steps to Forgiveness 13
Walking in Purpose 17
   Purpose 20
Walk in Victory 23
   Success 24
   Renew Your Mindset 27
   Renounce Old Environments 28
   Releasing a Sound 30
Share your Story 33
   From Mess to Message 37
Restoration 41
   Restoring Others 42
   Receive Instructions 43
   Eliminate Excuses 46
   Shut the Door 55
   Take Back Your Life 57
   Obtain Order 59
   Re-Write Your Story 61
   Execute the Plan 65

Plan	65
Prepare	65
Learning from Others	66
Adjustments	68
Navigating Through the Obstacles	69
Conclusion	71

INTRODUCTION

I was lying in bed one morning, and my mind went back to a conversation I had with a mentor friend of mine. She was telling me she was speaking to a person, and my name was brought up in the conversation. During the conversation, she began to tell this person how I have a strong testimony and I have experienced and overcome obstacles in my life. While she was talking, she said she began to give some example about me to the guy. In the process of her illustration, she stated she could tell the individual was completely clueless about the piece of information she was sharing with him. She stopped and asked this question of him "has he not shared this with you"? The guy responded, "No, I wasn't aware of any of this". She abruptly changed the subject, but in the back of her mind she thought, he hasn't shared his story.

I can clearly remember the conversation I had with her because it was one that brought liberty and rest to me. We were on the telephone having a mentor session, and she was talking to me about my goals in my life-coaching business. She asks me a question, and while I was getting my thoughts together to answer it, it was like she had an "ah-ha" moment. She interrupted me before I could answer, "Jarrod, do you not share your story with other people? You're ashamed of something that you are on the other side of." At that moment, I couldn't do anything but sit there because she apparently read my mail and articulated the emotions I had struggled with for years. For years, I had struggled with shame, guilt, and regrets of many things that had happened in my past. This phone call was a defining moment in my life. I will never forget it.

    Many people find it hard to overcome the scenes that plague their minds and interrupt their thoughts. Things such as people, places, and objects can trigger degrading moments, offense, and poor decision making of our past. These scary images can handicap us, and if we aren't careful, they can also lead us to an unproductive place. The thought of our past can take us somewhere we don't want to go and keep us longer than we want to stay

    If you are like many of the people we talk to on our jobs, listen to on the phone, and follow on social media who wrestle with their past mistakes and regrets, then this book is for you.

    In this book, you will receive principles that will encourage you to:

- Forgive yourself and others
- Walk in purpose

- Share your story
- Make your past your platform

CHAPTER ONE
FORGIVENESS

The word forgiveness is a popular term among many coaches, spiritual leaders, parents, and even physiologists. It is individual information received after a person has been hurt, scared, or terrified that can make or break the communication one has with him or herself. Although the term can be used for advice. The actual action and application have been challenging.

I wrestled with forgiveness for years. I not only wrestle with forgiving other, I also struggled with forgiving myself.

Merriam Webster dictionary defines forgiveness as "to give up resentment of or claim for requital". Strong's concordance defines forgiveness as "freedom, pardon, deliverance" 859(Greek). If we take the two definitions, we can see forgiveness means to release something. I believe the very reason some of us are angry and cynical can be traced back to past examples, which were offered to us or hurt us severally. Instead of releasing the experience, we held on to them. Instead of becoming better, we become bitter. We may not see it but people may not like to be around us, because we are constantly negative, and have nothing positive to say.

Steps to Forgiveness

Many people gain their inspiration from different sources. Some are inspired by successful leaders, philosophers, business owner, etc. I have also gained motivation and inspiration from various individuals in these fields. However, my greatest source of inspiration has come from an old book called the Bible. In this book, I have gained so much insight on how to be successful. One of the greatest pieces of advice has come from a man and prophet by the name of Isaiah. He spoke by inspiration of the Holy Spirit and said "Remember ye, not the former things, neither consider the things of old. Behold, I will do a new thing; now it shall spring forth; shall ye not know it?" I like the way it's explained in another version "Forget about what has happened; don't keep going over old history. Be alert, be present. I'm about to do something brand-new." Isa 43: MSG

1. Settle It

"Remember ye, not the former things, neither consider the things of old..." The text encourages us not to remember the things of the past. That is a bit challenging, to totally forget how bad others have treated, or misused you. How do you not remember being looked over or not even being considered? Is it possible not to remember the mistakes, regrets, and failure you have experienced?

The answer to the complicated question is YES! The way that you start this process is by settling something and then moving forward. You have to resolve your past. One day when I was sitting in a seminar, a teacher began to lecture on the definition of past and what it was. He gave an explanation that the past was a moment in time that no longer exists. I thought to myself "WOW."

I began to talk to myself, "I'm mad and upset about a moment in time that no longer exist." I was holding unforgiveness towards a moment in time that no longer existed.

Perhaps in reading this book right now you're asking yourself this question, "Am I withholding forgiveness towards a moments time that no longer exist?" There is something you must realize about the past; it is something that you have already overcome. My past has been a great classroom for me, whereby I have gained knowledge and wisdom. I don't know of anywhere else I could have received these valuable tools.

2. Law of Design

The law of design is a fundamental principle that must be understood if you are on the road to forgiveness. A law is a principle that you can expect to work the same way every time. The law of design simply states that you have been designed to move forward. Everything created has been designed to move forward. Take your body for example. Look at various parts. Were your arms designed to move backward? Were your eyes designed to look backward or forward? What about your legs? Were they created to go backward or to go forward? The point that I want to drive home with you is that regardless of the trials and tribulation you may have experienced, you were still designed to move forward.

After you have received the understanding that you have been designed to move forward, then it's time to move. You have to tell yourself daily that you were created to move forward. There are so many opportunities that await you as you begin to take your life back.

CHAPTER TWO

WALKING IN PURPOSE

Reflecting on my life, I must say that I have sat in some excellent classrooms. I have learned so much from my past. I read a quote one time that said "there is no such thing as failure, only feedback". I love this quote because it gives a positive perspective on life. The definition of feedback is, information about reactions to a product, or a person's performance of a task, etc., used as a basis for improvement. If you look at the definition, it tells us that feedback is for improvement. I honestly believe that I have gotten better because of the feedback of my past.

I think that while you are reading this book, you are getting better also knowing that your past can simply be used to make you better. How else would you know what a healthy relationship looks like if you didn't endure a bad one? How else would you know what it feels like to pass up opportunities if you didn't let a few slide? Some of us wouldn't know how to be a loving parent and respectful adult if we didn't encounter absentee love ones and rude authority figures. If we had never had the feedback, how would we compare life?

I remember seeking guidance from several respectable people in my life. There was a period in my life where I felt lied to and betrayed. In my distress, I was looking for some answer as to why certain things happen to me and what was the lesson behind it. Some of the greatest pieces of advice came from a respected leader by the name of Paul. He said "And we know that in all things God works for the good of those who love him, who have been called according to his purpose." I meditated on these words for years. I have come to a realization that everything that I have gone through good and bad, God can use it. Some may say "how can God use my terrible past"? Let me give you an example. I use to love watching my mom bake cakes. She would get all her ingredients out and lay them on the table in preparation to use them. If you were to take an inventory of the ingredients she used, there would be things such as butter, grease, vanilla extract, etc. If a person took those ingredients and ate them one by one, they would realize that if you eat those things individually, they are not pleasant or tasteful. Yet, if I take a bowl and put all of those ingredients in it one by one and began to blend them together until it becomes a smooth mixture, I can pour into a pan and stick it in an oven. The oven has a certain temperature that it must be on for the cake to cook. Once the cake has run its course in the oven, you pull it out, and it has become something desirable. Notice something; the cake could not have become profitable unless all the ingredients where used.

My belief is, if you did not experience the things of your past you would not be the person you are today, which includes your knowledge about life, wisdom, about situations and understanding that assist you in making right decisions. The writer said, "And we know that in all things God works"....

Purpose

If there has ever been a topic that I enjoy talking about, it would have to be the subject of purpose. My life completely changed when I began to realize that I was created on purpose and for a purpose. If we are going to have real confidence in who we are, we will have to grasp the concept of purpose. The greatest battle that you will fight is the fight of your past versus your present.

The definition of Purpose is the reason something exists. As I have quoted in many of my books, the late Myles Monroe once said: "when purpose isn't known abuse is inevitable." That only means that when you don't know your purpose, you harm yourself and other things. So many people have been stuck in the past because they don't understand what real purpose is. Understanding purpose will help us define the big picture. When an artist or an architect begin a project, they must first start with the big picture or the end results in mind. If the artist starts to paint or draw something other than what he has in mind because he has a reference point he can stop and start over to get back on track. For example, if the architect lays a wrong foundation or alters a measurement that puts something off track.

He has a point of reference to look at so that he can get back on track. Many people don't know where to look to because they never considered that when God created them, he designed them with the end in mind (Isaiah 46:10). God is so serious about the concept of purpose that before he creates anything he already knows the reason it will exist. For more on purpose check out my book "Purpose the reason for your existence."

My belief is that if you did not experience the things of your past you would not be the person you are today, which includes your knowledge about life, wisdom, about situations and understanding that assist you in making right decisions. The writer said, "And we know that in all things God works"….

CHAPTER 3

WALK IN VICTORY

Walking in victory is a mindset. So many times we allow our past experiences to be the model for the lifestyle that we live. We build a belief system off of the negative things in our lives, which is why at times we can't recognize the good things that come to us. For you to walk with victory in your life, you must first understand that you have been created to succeed. I know that may sound a little strange due to that fact that you are reading this book and trying to see what it takes to let go of the past. I want to inform you that God has built a blueprint for your life, and it is "Guaranteed to Success." I learned an important principle one day, and it has changed my life forever. I heard a man once say that God wants me to be successful because his reputation relies on it. I thought about it and said WOW!

Success

The man goes on and further explains about success, "success is always in the mind of the manufacturer." Let's evaluate this statement. We are in a technology age where many of us carry, or have inside our homes products manufactured by Apple. Everything Apple produces rests upon the logo on the product. The logo is the reputation of the company. Suppose you were to order an iPhone 7 from Apple. When the product arrives at your location, it will come in a box from the enterprise. When you open the box, the first thing you may come in contact with is a manual. The manual is nothing more than the instructions for the product. It informs you how the product operates. It gives the what, how, and why of the product. Inside this manual, there is a section that tells you the do's and don'ts of the product. It also says if the product malfunctions, not to try to fix it ourselves. The manual contains information as to where to send the product back at no cost. The reason we can ship the product back to the company at no expense is because the reputation of the enterprise is on the line. The company believes in the success of the product so much it is willing to sacrifice whatever it needs to for you to be satisfied with the product.

 This same illustration holds true with God. Success is always in the mind of God when he is creating anything. To show you this is true, let's look at the original story of humanity. Genesis 1:26 says "And God said, let us make man in our image, after our likeness…" Many of us do not read the manual, and in return, we receive minimum results.

In the creative process of humanity, the first thing God did when he created his product was to stamp it with his logo. Geneses 1:26 says "And God said, let us make man in our image. The fact that God has stamped us in the image of God is an indication success was always in the mind of God when he created us. You may be in a situation right now where it looks like your life is a failure. Being stamped with the image of God allows me to say, I have Good News, "You haven't failed because failing isn't an option when it comes to your life. God's image is his reputation because that is who he is. Everything God does rests upon who He is. God does mind putting his reputation on the line because he cannot fail.

The next thing God did to ensure our success was give us a manual. The manual provided to us is the Hebrew text call the Bible. Remember what I said earlier, the manual serves a great purpose as it pertains to the product. It gives us the understanding of the function of the product. What's sad is that many people don't take the time to read the manual, and in return, so many of us are receiving minimum results.

Keys to walking in victory
- Renew your mindset
- Renounce old environments and friends
- Release a sound

Let us examine each principle one by one.

Renew Your Mindset

To walk in victory requires a renewed mindset. The reason it needs a new mindset is that many of us may have a thought pattern that tells us that defeat is our final destination.

Paul, a first-century leader, quotes that we are not to be confirmed to the world, but we are to be transformed (changed) by the renewing of the mind. The principle for real transformation lies in this quote. For change to come, one must renew their mind. It's imperative for us to gain an understanding of what it means to renew something. The term "renew" can be defined as to make new or re-do. It's also translated or substituted with the word renovate. I'm sure that many of us are familiar with this term. To renovate something means to take out old junk and replace it with new valuables. For us to walk victoriously, it's imperative that we remove and replace our old mindset and belief system that is contrary to the place we are pursuing. We must get rid of the stinking thinking.

Renounce Old Environments

Out of the three steps, this one has the potential of being the hardest. The reason being is that anytime you have been connected to or involved with people, places, or things for a period; you run a risk of becoming attached to it. When you are attached to something that very thing can be something that you depend on to provide you the essential of life. Being disconnected from it can become very dangerous, especially if your mind isn't made up to stay away.

What most people don't realize is that your environment is critical to your success. When talking about the environment, I like to use metaphors to bring my point across. If you were to take a fish out of the water and place it on the ground, what would happen to the fish? If you were to uproot a plant and take it out of the ground and put it in muddy water what would happen to the plant? The point that I'm trying to drive home is that it is very crucial that you be in the right environment.

Many of the environments that we choose to

become familiar with are so toxic that it is the very instrument that stops us from dreaming, hoping, and pursuing what is best for our lives. That same environment has told us that we will never amount to anything. It has whispered in your ear and said that you can only reach a certain level in life. It has also encouraged you to live an average and mediocre life, which is far below your potential. We must renounce this thing immediately. According to Merriam's dictionary, the term "renounce" means

"to refuse to follow, obey, or recognize any further". For us to be truly useful at this stage, we must first acknowledge and accept everything that we have spoken about up until this point.

    I can relate to so many people on this level because of what I have experienced in my life. After being released from prison, one of my many challenges was wondering if the people, places, and things of my former life would receive me for who I was now. I had to be convinced of my transformation. If I doubted it, I could have returned to my former lifestyle. This lifestyle included a toxic environment with unhealthy people and relation-ships. Returning would have been the result of looking for validation in something that I should have renounced.

Releasing a Sound

A vital key to walking in victory is learning how to release a sound. To release a sound just means that you are to open your mouth and say something. You don't have a right to remain silent if you are to live victoriously. When pursuing victorious living, one of the temptations that we will face is that certain things will contradict what we are pursuing. When facing these obstacles, sometimes we have a tendency to remain silent. Your past will always present itself to you-begging and pleading to let it come back into your life. It may come in the form of friends, activities, environments, nick-names, etc. I have experienced this many times. I can vividly remember one situation. I made contact with a friend that I hadn't talked to in many years. I was excited about speaking to them. While we were on the phone, they started going down memory lane. Keep in mind that with most people, if they haven't grown up, they will always try to relate to you on the level they first meet you. The reason people do this is because they have taken an inspection of their life and have come to the conclusion that change isn't possible. They attempt to justify accepting the stagnation of their life by making statements like "I'm just me", "I have to be real with myself". On this particular day while we were talking, this person began to call me by my old nicknames and relate to me by past faults and failures. When we finished talking, I finally hung the phone up, and those old images were still in my mind. I could see myself involved with the activity. I realized the conversation conjured up emotions. I also realized these emotions had to come from somewhere. They were coming from my thoughts. At that moment, I had to open my mouth and say something. I said, "Jarrod Dunn, you are not that person, you are a man of integrity, you live victoriously, and your past is dead." After that day, I realized how serious it was. I made a decision from that day forward to never keep my mouth shut when I am challenged to revert to something I have renounced.

CHAPTER 4

SHARE YOUR STORY

Let Your Past Be Your Platform

Often when people overcome things in life they keep it to themselves not realizing that it could be the very thing that helps others to overcome. I stated at the beginning of the book, that I was talking to my mentor one day, and she helped uncover some hidden things inside of me. I remember one morning when I went to school with my son, because they were having an all-pro dad meeting. In this session, many fathers would bring their children into a room and they would bond with them before school. On this particular day, the administrator of this program began to ask the children what was their favorite Christmas memory. As each child took a turn explaining their favorite memories. I started to become nervous and saying to myself "I hope my son doesn't say his most memorable Christmas was when his dad came home from prison." If you were wondering if he said it, he didn't. On this particular day, my life changed. After the conversation that I had with my mentor, I was exposed and knew I had to do something about it.

There are many examples that we could follow as it pertains to people that have bounced back from setbacks. If I was not open to the instruction that I received, I wouldn't be able to pen this book, speak with clarity and boldness, and say my message, which is "your past doesn't have to define you." I know first-hand how people try to keep you in your past. It's amazing how something that no longer exists can still be a reality if you don't come to grips with the fact that you may have done, engaged, and experienced some things in life, but you don't have to identify yourself with the negative aftereffect.

If I could turn back the hands of time and speak to some of the world's greatest leaders such as Martin Luther King, Mother Teresa, Nelson Mandela, Corey Ten Boom, etc. I would ask them how they developed their message. I can almost promise you all of them would say their message came from things they experienced and overcame.

Martin Luther King had many words that he delivered during a time where blacks were experiencing harsh punishment and injustice. They were being beaten, killed, put in jail, etc. The oppression was so cruel and unfair that many were tempted to give up and stop moving forward. The Message Dr. King spoke was a message he developed through his life experience. He clearly understood that if the people gave up now, they would fall short of equality. One of his greatest quotes, "If you can't fly, then run, if you can't run, then walk, if you can't walk, then crawl, but whatever you do, you have to keep moving forward", was spoken during these challenging times.

Mother Teresa is known as one of the greatest contributors to this world that we have seen. Her story is remarkable!! In her autobiography, she talks about how she was working at a school in Calcutta India. To get to work each day she had to walk. She talked about how every day she would have to step over dead, deserted and homeless people. One day she said that she couldn't take it anymore, so Mother Teresa went to her Priest and asked for her check because she was quitting. He replied "you're quitting, for what" Mother Teresa went on to explain that she was taking her check and going downtown to buy some food to feed the homeless. The priest tried to reassure her that she was making a mistake by quitting, because her check wasn't enough money to feed the millions of homeless people that were on the street of Calcutta. Mother Teresa again demanded her check and told him that her check may not be enough to feed the million, but it was sufficient to feed one. That is why she had a message that said: "If you can't feed a hundred people, then just feed one." Her message derived from an experience that she overcame.

Nelson Mandela, the former South African president, spent 27 years in prison for fighting an unjust system. His family was also suffering harm from outside forces. You would think a man who had spent the majority of his life incarcerated would have just given up and blamed others for his misfortune. He didn't, he became the president of South Africa and lived a life of forgiveness. He truly exemplified how to let the past be a platform not a stumbling block.

From Mess to Message

We took a journey and looked at many of our greatest leaders, and we have seen that a lot of their messages derived from a mess. It's great to know that our mess doesn't have to have the final words on our life.

The question we have to ask ourselves today is, what do you have to say about your situation? You'll be surprised at the many people that have gone through the same things as you, but they are still stuck looking for someone like you to help them. 1 Corinthians 10:13 (MSG) 13 "No test or temptation that comes your way is beyond the course of what others have had to face". This passage of scripture says that there is no test, nor temptation that you have gone through that is different from someone else's. The difference in you is that you now have an understanding that enables you to let your past be your platform from which you help others.

What will you say to others? Maybe you are like countless others, that have been without a parent or real authority figure in their life. Will you play the victim role and constantly be in rebellion against those that are in charge? Will you be someone always looking for others to give you something without hard work, because you feel like someone owes you something? Perhaps people in past relationships have used and abused you. Will you continually ruin loving and caring people because you deal with the pain from past hurt and frustration? The alternative to the victim role is the victor role. The "victor" is someone that has gone through many obstacles. Instead of letting the obstacles ruin their life, they choose to live a life that says "I may have been effected by the situation, but I refuse to let this determine my life" WOW! That's the mindset

What do you have to say about your story? Will you share it with others or will you just keep it in like I did for many years? The moment I began to release it I became free from my past.

CHAPTER 5

RESTORATION

In this chapter, I'm going to give you guidance on how to be restored. I also used these same tools in my restoration process. There are two types of people in the world deliverers and captives. Deliverers help set the captives free.

It has brought me great joy throughout the years as I tell my story to others and see their faces light up. For some odd reason, we have a tendency to think that we are the only one to go through something so severe in life that others can't relate. I read an article in my favorite book that said "He that waters shall also be watered himself (Proverbs 11:25). The Proverbs writer explains to us a vital principle. He tells us that for us to get we must give. There may be something that you are seeking to receive inside of your life at this juncture. You may be in need of encouragement, opportunities, love, mercy, and compassion. I have learned that if I would open my mouth and allow myself to be available to others, then the very things that are needed personally will be given unto me as I give it to others.

Restoring Others

When you begin the restoring process, keep in mind that it's a two-way street. The process can't be one-sided. There has to be willingness from both parties. If one-person commits and the other doesn't, you will have a tedious project. The second thing to keep in mind is that you have remembered that you at one time were in the restoration seat, so there is no room for arrogance and pride. I have a low tolerance for the people that act like they have always had it together. That attitude will restrict you from making an impact on anyone's life.

According to dictionary.com, the word restore means to put back to a former place, or to a former position, rank, etc. In this process, I like to use the acronym from the word R-E-S-T-O-R-E. We will explore each letter and learn the principle behind it. Remember that I'm talking from a perspective of helping or coaching others to being restored in this chapter. Also, you may be saying I need restoration myself.

The principle that I'm sharing in these sections are life changing and can be applied by anyone looking for victory.

<u>R</u>ESTORE

Receive Instructions

The letters R in the word restore stands for receive instructions. It's crucial during this stage you begin the process by receiving instructions. Helping others and yourself to be brought back to a healthy place requires proper instructions. You may think you have a plan that's ready to be implemented. You might have an attitude that says I know what to do. Please keep in mind the words of a wise man that says "Plans fail for lack of counsel, but with many advisers, they succeed." (Prov. 15:22). Your ability to receive instruction in the situation is crucial. At this stage, you must make sure you are in a place where you can get proper instructions.

Steps to receiving instruction

1. Prayer

During this time of restoration, prayer is vital. Because your total dependency isn't about you and your experience, it's in God's ability to provide you with whatever you need to get the job done. The proverb writer instructs us to "Trust God from the bottom of your heart". Don't try to figure out everything on your own. Listen to God's voice in everything you do; everywhere you go; he's the one who will keep you on track. Don't assume that you know it all. (Proverbs 3:5-6 MSG)

2. Listening (meditating)

In this stage listening is critical. You must be in a place where you can listen to the instruction so that you will have the right method to help yourself and others. If I come to you for an answer and we are in a conversation; and I'm the one doing all the talking, how can I receive anything from you. The old saying is true in this situation; "we have two ears for listening and one mouth for talking. Let me just clear something up here about listening. "Don't look for an audible voice." Pay attention to the environment; see how things are forming and most important follow the peace. The first-century church leader, Paul the apostle, in-structs a group of individuals on the proper order of making a sound decision. He say's "and let the peace (soul harmony which comes) from Christ rule (act as umpire continually) in your hearts [deciding and settling with finality all questions that arise in your minds, in that peaceful state] to which as [members of Christ's] one body you were also called [to live]. And be thankful (appreciative),[giving praise to God always]." (Amp)

3. Application

After you have prayed and then listen to the

instruction, then it is time for the final stage, application. Applying can be difficult for some people. The reason it is challenging is that people will pray and listen, but they have trouble with applying. When I think about this stage, I'm reminded of the words of Mary, who informed the apostle after they were trying to find a solution to a problem. She looked at them and said, "Whatever he tells you to do, do it." Whatever you think you are supposed to do, please do it. Let's make something clear because I have seen some people get into some weird things. Make sure that what you think you are supposed to do is in order. There is nothing wrong with consulting with someone and asking them for advice.

RESTORE

Eliminate Excuses

Excuses are the nails that built the house of failure -
Unknown

Whenever you reach the point of restoration, one of your greatest enemies will be your excuses. These opponents will try to present themselves because they don't want you to move forward. Excuses will try to justify why you can't do something or the reason you can't accomplish it. You have to view them as your archenemy. According to the online etymology dictionary, the word excuse comes from two words. One example, which means outward or external. The second word is cuss which means, "troublesome person or animal," an alteration of the word curse. (www.etymonline.com/). Curse means according to Merriam dictionary, "a solemn utterance intended to invoke a supernatural power to inflict harm or punishment on someone or something." If you put the two words together they mean an external curse, something formed on the outside to harm you. The curse or excuse is something that is said. Every time you allow an excuse to come out of your mouth, you are hurting yourself. Most people don't realize excuses will do more outward damage to a person than they realize. Every time a person speaks why they can't do something, or the reason they are not doing something, they are doing harm to their progress.

Eliminate excuses

Being restored relies on an individual realizing that excuses are one of the many factors that can hinder their success. I want to share with you five principles on how to deal with excuses.

Let's take the acronym of excuse and learn from it.

<u>EX</u>CUSE

1. Examine Yourself - When dealing with excuses, the first step you must take is to examine why you have an excuse for this particular situation. Many times the excuses come from a belief system developed from people, experiences, etc. View the example below to see how a belief system can be formed.

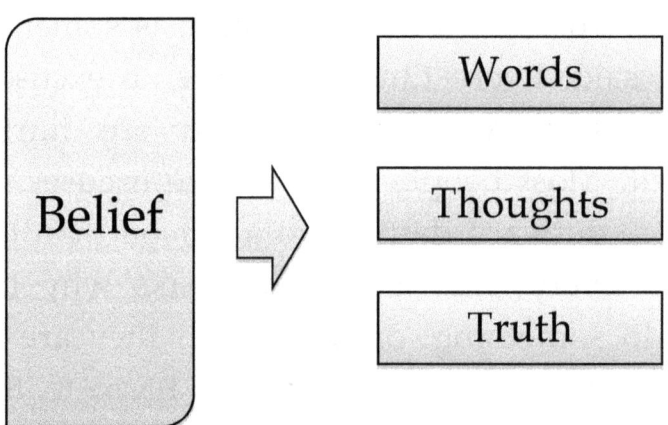

Three things always develop a belief system. Those three things are words, thoughts, and truth. Whenever you begin to believe something is when it first starts in the mind. Thoughts come into the formation by what's said. When something is said, you make it an idea. The way you make it an idea is by meditating on it. Meditate means, according to freedictionary.com, "to plan in the mind; intend: To think or reflect, especially in a calm and deliberate manner."Reflect on your experience and every time someone said something to you that was totally against your future. When people told you that you weren't smart enough. There might have been those that said that you would never amount to anything. Some could have said that you weren't going to be successful. Somewhere along the line, you believe them. The reason I know that you have accepted and settled for what others have said is by your excuses. Excuses or an outward expression of the truth you believe. Once the word becomes thought and you have meditated on them, they become truth to you. For thoughts to become reality, you have to accept or settle the things you have been meditating on in your mind.

You can always tell if a person has decided something in their mind, it will be displayed through their actions. The truth will empower you. "What you believe will determine what you say, what you say will determine what you do. When you start making excuses, examine and ask yourself why? Why am I saying this, why do I believe that?

EXCUSE

2. Cancel Out Negative Thoughts - The second principle in dealing with excuses is to cancel out the negative thoughts. The way you cancel out negative thought is by capturing it when it occurs. To capture something means to take captive, as by force or craft; seize: to gain possession or control of. Excuses are dangerous. Being restored carries with it a deep sense of responsibility. You must capture the negativity that tries to invade your life. You can't afford to let such thoughts linger in your mind.

EXCUSE

3. Utilize your Confession - The third thing you must do in confronting your excuses is use positive con-fession. Most people don't understand the power of their confession. I gained this revelation one day when I was reading my favorite book. In the eleventh chapter and sixteenth verse of Hebrews, it said, "By faith we understand that the worlds [during the successive ages] were framed (fashioned, put in order, and equipped for their intended purpose) by the word of God, so that what we see was not made out of things which are visible (amplified)." This Hebrew writer said that God created the worlds, not by a hammer, saw, or bulldozer, etc. He created the worlds by his words. The words that he spoke formed into existence the very things that we are living in today. Our words have the same ability to create the very world that we live in. The world that you are living in currently is probably a replica of what you have spoken out of your mouth. Take some time out and make a list of some positive things that you would like to see in our life. Your confession may not happen over-night. If you continue to confess it, then it won't to be long before you see it. The reason I know this is right is that it goes back to what you believe. The more I confess it, the more I hear it. Sooner or later because I regularly speaking it, then I will settle it as truth. Once the truth is settling then here, comes the action. I'm excited about your confession!!!

EXCUSE

4. Start - The fourth step in dealing with excuse sounds so easy, but yet it is hard for many people to accomplish. This principle is called the power of start. Once you have examined yourself, canceled out the negative thoughts, utilized your con-fession, now it is time to start moving in the direction that your excuse is trying to keep you from. The power of start is just action. If you are going to be successful in this section of your life, you must start. If you don't start then, nothing changes. Everything will remain the same.

EXCUSE

5. Encourage Yourself - The final step in eliminating excuses is to encourage yourself. There will be times during this process when you are tempted to go backward. At times, things may also look as if they are not working. Please do not give up. In this process you will realize that you may not have many cheerleaders and your number one fan will probably be you. Encourage yourself.

If you are going to be successful in carrying out your assignment, then you are going to have to learn to talk to yourself. I know that may sound a little strange to some people, but to those that have ever been alone in life, depending on others to help them; they quickly discover that those others counted on are nowhere to be found. You probably understand what I'm explaining. There will come a time in your life where you feel like you are going to need others and they aren't going to be there. At this moment, you are going to have to learn to talk to yourself. I'm not talking

Restoration

about just babbling out something or even disrespecting yourself. I'm talking about learning how to encourage and pump yourself up. I'm simply saying that no one can encourage you like you can. Tell yourself that you can do it. Use what fuel for the fire that you may need until you begin to see the results that you desire? Let me give you a word that will refresh you in this period of your life.

Let's examine someone who was an excellent example of this principle. 1 Samuel 30:6 says "And David was greatly distressed: for the people spoke of stoning him, because the soul of all the people was grieved, every man for his son and for his daughter but David encouraged himself in the Lord of his God." Let me give you some history. The setting of this scripture picks up in a confusing moment of David's life. David had experienced one of the greatest victories in the history of his nation. This young warrior had defeated a giant by the name of Goliath. Everybody is talking about what has happen. This young warrior is the topic of every conversation in the household of many. They are talking about how he has saved Israel from the Philistines. During this time, David could have been easily tempted to let pride overtake him, but

53

instead he returned home and enlist in the army of his king and served him faithfully. The young warrior served the king faithfully and helped the army of Israel win victory after victory. David noticed that the one he loves and has served with honesty has become jealous of him. King Saul constructs a plan to kill David, but the king's son Jonathan wasn't going to allow this to happen, so he informs David of his father's plan. When David received the news, he flees for his life and lands himself in the cave of Adullam. It was this cave that scripture states everyone that was in distress, in debt, and discontented, gathered themselves unto him: and he became a captain over them: in all there were with him about four hundred men (1 Samuel 22:2). It was at this place that David was able to connect himself with men who finally believed in him. The same group of men that we talked about David leading was the same group of men in the 30th chapter. David and his men had left their families and belongings behind to go and fight in a war. Upon returning home, they were surprised to see that villains had raided them. The villains had burned their homes and took their families. These men who believed in David now found themselves in a position of wanting answers to why this was

Restoration

happening. Instead of coming to their leader and asking him what to do, the text reveals to us that they turned on him and talked about killing him because they were so angry. This was challenging for David because this was a group of men who trust him and he felt like he had let them down. Instead of giving up, he did something life changing. The scripture said, "David encouraged himself in the Lord of his God." According to Strong's Concordance #2388, The word encouraged means -to strengthen, cure, help, or repair. If we were to take these words and replace them in the scripture, it would read "David strengthened, cured, helped, repaired himself in the Lord of his God. Wow!! This text shows us clearly how encouraging yourself will help you overcome obstacles.

RE<u>S</u>TORE

SHUT The Door

So many people relapse and go back and entangle themselves with unproductive things because they don't shut the doors in their life. Doors can represent many things. One thing that they illustrate is access. When my door is open often times it means that I've given you permission to comes in. With that permission, it also offers entrance and exposure into my world.

In order for a person to be restored and brought to a productive place, this is a valuable principle to learn. Shutting the door on past relationships, activities, thought patterns, etc. is a must. I mentioned previously that your past will always come knocking at your door. The reason it wants back in is because it doesn't like you moving forward. You must understand that if the door is shut it is closed for a reason. Keep in mind that only you have the power to open or close the doors of your past.

I have heard people say they thank God for open doors. I thank God for open doors also. I also thank God for closing doors. The reason why closed doors are so important to me is that I no longer have a desire to go back to the door being closed. I may be tempted to go back but just seeing the door closed is a reminder that I no longer have access to that arena. One of my favorite artist has a song that says "I'm not going back, I'm moving ahead, here to declare to You my past is over in You All things are made new, surrendered my life to Christ I'm moving, moving forward" These words are powerful. You have to shut the doors to your past, and as we have just explained in the previous chapter you have declared that it is over!!

Closing the doors are crucial, you have to make the decision that you are going to shut them and that they will remain locked at all times.

RESTORE

TAKE BACK YOUR LIFE

At this stage of the restoration process, It's important that you get your mind and emotions together. Now that you have taken the steps up to this point, the next phase is crucial in order for you to move forward. This is the stage in your life where you are going to have to fight!! It's time to "Take back your life"

When we began the journey of taking our life back we have to keep in mind that you can only take back what is legally yours. I have seen many people develop an attitude that says if it's for me then God will bless me with it, or if it's for me then I'll get it. I do agree with this statement to some extent, however, if we will be honest with ourselves most of the time when we say things like that we are really saying "if it happens it happen, but I'm not going to put any effort in it". This mindset puts the whole responsibility on God and others but it excludes self from any effort.

The term take means according to the freedictionary.com; to seize with authority or legal right. You have a legal right to seize what is yours with authority. Take an inventory of your life and look at the things that have been stolen from you. The thief may have come in a form of a negative relationship that you invested time in but in return receive nothing but calamity and misfortune. It may have shown up as an authority figure that spoke something terrible in your life and you believed the lie. The lie since then has played in your mind like a broken record allowing you to only believe certain things and reject others.

Today is a new day for you. It's imperative you receive this message. As I pen these words I'm reminded of the time I had to take my life back. I was labeled as a menace to society by a federal judge. I was told all my life that I would be like family members that were great people relationally but displayed poor morality. I had a speech impediment that caused others to laugh at me but left me with low self-esteem. I was told that my smile was ugly, so in return I would put my hand over my mouth every time I thought something was funny. One day while looking in the mirror I said to myself "enough is enough". I'm going to love me for me regardless of what others may think. I used the critics and the haters for fuel. When I thought about giving up, I would remember what others had said about me and how they tried to count me out but I kept going. I took my life back. The more I continued to move forward, the more I was empowered. Your life is too powerful for you to allow something or someone to be in control of it.

RESTORE

Obtain Order

In the restoration process, order is valuable. When you don't have an understanding of order, then dysfunction becomes the norm for your life. Order is a standard or code of conduct that is put in place for the purpose of productivity. A person can lose it all if they don't understand what order is or looks like. Order is what will keep things intact. When you are in a process of restoring, you have to have a gauge because if not you will begin to depend on your best thinking. I like to tell people that my best thinking has gotten me into many troubles. There was a point in my life that I thought order was what I saw in my home and community. Don't misunderstand me, I learned some treasured lessons, but I also learned some valuable ones. Your success shouldn't be measured by how many have failed in your family or community. Success should be measured by the standard of what Christ has said about your victory.

According to the online etymology dictionary, the term order, means Latin ordinem (nominative ordo) "row, rank, series, arrange-ment, it is also from Italic root *ord- "to arrange, the arrange-ment." You see that the word order has something to do with the rank or arrangement of something. If we are going to allow our past to be our platform, we will have to learn how to arrange somethings in our life. The way to arrange them is that you place them in the order of importance. You have to prioritize them according to the level of importance. Let me make this very clear. When you're at this point in your life, you must realize that your horizontal relationship will affect you unilaterally.

Some of you are reading this asking what I mean. The relationship you have with God, which is upward, will change the relationship that you have with yourself and others across the board. The right order exists when you recognize the most important things and strategically place them in the rank of importance. Make a list and record the top five things in your life. Take that same list and begin to create a plan of action for each one.

RESTORE

RE-WRITE YOUR STORY

Re-writing your story is something that you rarely hear people talk about. I don't know if most people have developed a mindset that says "I made my bed and now I have to lay in it" this quote tells a person that no matter what they have done, they have to deal with it. I agree with this statement to some degree. There may have been somethings that I have gone through in my life that I have to accept responsibility for, however, I am the writer of my story, and I will determine how it will end.

I remember speaking at an event and when I finished talking about my particular topic the host of the event was excited, and he said, "Who will you play in your movie"? That's a vital question that you must ask yourself. Will you play the victim who is always pointing the finger at someone? The victim is constantly blaming other for why things are not the way they want them to be. Will you play the successful one? The successful one is the hero of the movie that overcomes the obstacles that they face. Regardless of what you have experienced up until this point you have to realize that you are the only one that has the final say so.

How to Re-Write the Story

Re-writing your story requires a few simple steps. They may be simple, but they are critical to your story.

1. Visualize - The first thing that a person needs to do is to visualize how they want their story to go. Being able to visualize is paramount when you are rewriting your story. According to dictionary.com, visualize means 'to make perceptible to the mind or imagination'.

Visualization has everything to do with an individual using their mind to paint a mental image of a person, place, or thing. When you begin to re-write your story, you have to get the concept in your mind on what role you and others will play in your story. In your story will you play the victim, an impotent, weak, individual who points the finger at others while they continue to be walked over. Will you play the hero? The hero is the one who faces the obstacles, trials, and setbacks and overcomes them because he or she realizes that they have been created to live above the circumstance and not beneath.

2. Write it down - After you have visualized your story, it is important to note that this is your story and not someone else's opinion about your life. I would hope that you would not conceive something that is far below your potential.

Writing your story is not the same as goal setting. There is a big difference between your goals and what you visualize. Goals are specific and quantifiable. They have an endpoint. Once you've achieved a goal, you're done with it. Goals tell us what we need to do to get to the desired outcome. A vision, on the other hand, is a broad, all-encompassing idea of how you want your life to look, feel, and be in the future. When you close your eyes and imagine your ideal life, that's vision. Unlike goals, it's open-ended. There's never a particular moment when you can say, "I achieved my vision." This is why it is critical to writing you goals down and allow them to be at a location where you can see them daily. I like what one man said to another. He said, "What you look at consistently will become reality."

3. Action - In re-writing your story, this is one of the most important steps. Many people are all right up until they get to this point, the reason being is that it requires them to do something. After you have the vision, write it down, now it's time to put some feet on it. You have to get moving. In this stage, there are a few things that you must determine. What you must establish is who, what, and how. The 'who' deals with the people. Who will be involved with helping your story become fact and not fiction? Who will have lead roles in your story? These are things that you must figure out. The next thing is the 'what'. What will it take for me to allow these people to be a part of my life? That's a valid question because you play a significant role in bringing all this together. Also, what are the necessary steps that we must take to accomplish this vision? The final ingredient is the 'how'. The 'how' is important because this is what will enhance your ability to act. "The distance between your dreams and reality is called action."

RESTOR<u>E</u>

Execute the Plan

Executing the plan is one of the most tedious and challenging things that people pursue. Now that you have visualized and written the plan down, it's time to Execute. This is the point most people get confused or quit. The reason being is because they don't have a plan. I heard a person quote, "a man who doesn't have a plan is a man who plans to fail". We've come too far now; so failing isn't an option let's get a plan together.

PLAN

Prepare
Learn from others
Adjustments
Navigate through the obstacles

Let's examine each one.

<u>P</u>LAN

Prepare

Now that you're at this stage of executing your plan, you will have to make sure that you are prepared. I had this one guy that I would see often, and every time he would come to me, he would always say "don't get ready be ready" what he was saying is be prepared. I've missed many opportunities in life because I wasn't prepared. Opportunities are waiting on your preparation. To be prepared only means to have a plan of action... Notice that I said a plan of ACTION. Many people have plans, but they don't have action. We talked about action in the last chapter.

Preparation is vital. The way you prepare is by understanding where you want to go and getting the right tools, skills, and people that will help you get there. There were times in my life I thought I was ready after I had a setback. The reason I wasn't able to come back as I expected was because I wasn't prepared. Take the necessary steps that are needed for you to be ready.

P_LAN

Learning from Others

Now that you are in the preparation phase and you understand how important it is to be ready. The L in plan stands for learning from other. In executing your plan, you must learn from others who have overcome the same

Restoration

obstacles. I know we like to think sometimes we are the only one that has gone through some cruel things. I have news for you; you're not the only one that has gone through something dramatic. There are some people who have experienced some horrific things and have overcome them to such a degree you could not even tell they had experienced anything.

Do not think you can execute a plan without consulting others. I can remember going through something's in my life I had never experienced before. I knew I had a plan to overcome it. I was taking the necessary steps to prepare myself for victory, but I didn't have the experience, or the wisdom, to apply what was needed to be successful. I contacted my mentor who had an excellent reputation, and he instructed me on the steps I needed to take to get the outcome I was looking for. I had to humble myself and seek counsel because I came to grips with the fact that I didn't know everything. Learning from others is key for being effective in executing your game plan

PL<u>A</u>N

Adjustments

At this juncture, you will have to learn to make the changes. Adjustments are central when you are working a plan. If you have ever set yourself out to do anything, you know sometimes plans don't go as followed. Things happen in life. Although things do occur in life, we should not deviate from the plan. We might have to take different roads or even change the vehicle on our way there, but we don't stop. We make the adjustments needed for us to get back on track. You may have a plan right now on what you are going to do and how you are going to do it. That is good. Don't be afraid to make an adjustment.

I've seen marriages; ministries, business, etc. fail all because they were not willing to make an adjustment. It may not even have to be something major, it may be something so simple as replacing one person or getting rid of an unproductive habit. You'd be surprised how it will sometimes be the little foxes that spoil the vine. Take a complete evaluation of your whole life. This includes relationships; finances, daily routines, etc. ask yourself the 'what' questions

1. What's going on around me? This mean you

need to observe what's going on around you positive or negative and recognize the role you play.

2. What's going on behind me? This only means you should take a look at anything you may be dealing with in the past that is holding you from reaching success in the future.

3. What's going on beside me? This means you take an inventory of anything you are connected with and determine if it will promote you or demote you.

4. What's going on inside me? Are there any emotions you may be dealing with which are toxic and can hinder you from moving forward? When you finish answering the questions, then you have to ask yourself what adjustments you need to make to get in line with the plan. Don't hesitate to write it down and keep it with you as a reminder.

PLA<u>N</u>

Navigating Through the Obstacles

The final step in executing the plan is navigating through the obstacles. We all like to think once we have a plan and we are about to execute it, everything will be smooth sailing. I hate to burst your bubble, that is not how it is.

Although we wish it were like that, you have to realize, anytime you are pursuing your dreams, they will be tested. You are on a journey of restoration. On this voyage, you will have to learn how to navigate through things. According to freedictionary.com, navigate means to plan and direct the course of a vessel or vehicle. This word is commonly used and associated with sailing. When a captain of a ship set out to sail a boat they already have the plan and the course in mind. During this voyage many things can appear on their way to the destination. Storms, hurricanes, troubles, sickness, etc. can be some of the challenges a sailor faces. Although they face the dilemma, a sailor knows he still has to navigate through to reach his place of destiny.

    To be restored and work the plan you have constructed, you must navigate through life challenges and temptations and always re-mind yourself you can't stop because you have a date with destiny.

Let Your Past Be Your Platform

CONCLUSION

Let Your Past Be Your Platform

I know many people are reading this book and probably asking themselves what gives me the authority to write a book like this.

My life has not always been peaches and cream. At the age of 10 I knew I had something great to pursue in life. When that revelation came to me, then life challenges and interruptions broke loose in my life. At the age of 13, I was living a fast and unrestrained lifestyle. I was looking for anything, trying everything because I lack direction in life. I grew up around the neighborhood drug dealers, local hustlers, and convicts. I wasn't afraid to live on the edge. I was not afraid to try new things even if I risked losing my life. Growing up in this environment put the image in my mind about life. It taught me everything I knew about getting over on others at the expense of me getting what I wanted. They told me I was cool. They said I could be good at making a living getting over on others. I bought into the lies I was told.

In 2004 I found myself along with others inside of a federal police car on my way to prison for a very long time. On my first offense, I was charged with manufacturing and distributing drugs. The judge slammed the gavel and gave me 145 months, this is 12 years. I thought my life was over.

Conclusion

At 21-years-old and newly married. My wife and I had two daughters, ages 3 and 1. On top of that, we were expecting a little boy. I felt like this was my worst nightmare.

During my incarceration, I found myself wrestling with frustrating days, confused and lonely nights. The prison was a jungle. There are things that went on that if I spoke about them people wouldn't believe me. Let's please don't forget to mention how humiliating it was. It was nothing but the power of God that allowed me to get through this horrific time in my life.

I was released in 2012. This was challenging for me. I'm so thankful my wife and family provided an easy transition for me. I can't help but think of where I would be if I didn't have that support. I immediately hit the ground running. I must say, it wasn't easy. I was considered a felon in a society where people looked down on you. I was determined not to allow their opinion to affect me. I began speaking and teaching all around East Tennessee and various states. I wrote books, started a business, and got involved in my community. I also became a pastor and leader to a great group of individuals. During the process, I realized doors were opening, and I was given the opportunity to sit at the table of great men and

Let Your Past Be Your Platform

women. What was it that allows a country boy from Tennessee to be around men and women that dominate their arena? I can't help but think I allowed my past to be my platform. A platform is something that gives you the opportunity to showcase who you are and what you can do. I took that mentality and used it for a place to help others know you don't have to allow your past to define you. I spoke with boldness, explained principles with clarity, and pursued to help others be restored. I walked in my purpose because I realized I was forgiven and in return I wanted other to forgive themselves. In a society that looks down on others because of mistakes, mishaps, and misfortunes. I have been talked about, criticized for being too young to do what I was doing. I have also been told by other leaders I respected deeply that I didn't deserve to be doing what I was doing because of my past. I didn't let it affect me. I used it as a platform to let others know your past doesn't have to define you. I thank God he has enlightened me to realize my past has the ability to propel me into my future. It is my hopes you have digested the principles I put in this book, because it has been the very thing I have used to help me overcome the four-letter word called "past".

Purchase your copy of "Let Your Past be your Platform" Today at Amazon.com

If you have been inspired by this book and would like more resources contact us at jdinnovation@yahoo.com.

For speaking engagements, workshop and seminars contact 423.457.9542

www.ingramcontent.com/pod-product-compliance
Lightning Source LLC
Chambersburg PA
CBHW071746040426
42446CB00012B/2481